HARRY STYLES
Making a Difference as a Singer

By Katie Kawa

KidHaven
PUBLISHING

People Who Make a Difference

Published in 2025 by
KidHaven Publishing, an Imprint of Greenhaven Publishing, LLC
2544 Clinton St.
Buffalo, NY 14224

Designer: Deanna Lepovich
Editor: Katie Kawa

Photo credits: Cover Debby Wong/Shutterstock.com; p. 5 Matt Crossick/Alamy Stock Photo; pp. 7, 9, 20 Featureflash Photo Agency/Shutterstock.com; pp. 11, 13 UPI/Alamy Stock Photo; p. 15 Fred Duval/Shutterstock.com; p. 17 (main) lev radin/Shutterstock.com; p. 17 (inset) Jeff Gilbert/Alamy Stock Photo; p. 18 Katrina Young/Alamy Stock Photo; p. 21 T.Sumaetho/Shutterstock.com.

Library of Congress Cataloging-in-Publication Data

Names: Kawa, Katie, author.
Title: Harry Styles : making a difference as a singer / Katie Kawa.
Description: [First.] | Buffalo, New York : KidHaven Publishing, 2024. |
   Series: People who make a difference | Includes index.
Identifiers: LCCN 2024009511 | ISBN 9781534548169 (library binding) | ISBN
   9781534548152 (paperback) | ISBN 9781534548176 (ebook)
Subjects: LCSH: Styles, Harry, 1994–Juvenile literature. |
   Singers–England–Biography–Juvenile literature. | LCGFT: Biographies.
Classification: LCC ML3930.S89 K38 2024 | DDC 782.42166092
   [B]–dc23/eng/20240301
LC record available at https://lccn.loc.gov/2024009511

Printed in the United States of America

Some of the images in this book illustrate individuals who are models. The depictions do not imply actual situations or events.

CPSIA compliance information: Batch #CSKH25: For further information contact Greenhaven Publishing LLC at 1-844-317-7404.

Please visit our website, www.greenhavenpublishing.com. For a free color catalog of all our high-quality books, call toll free 1-844-317-7404 or fax 1-844-317-7405.

Find us on

CONTENTS

A POWERFUL VOICE

Harry Styles has been in the spotlight for more than a decade. First as a member of the popular boy band One Direction and then as a **solo** star, he's found fame around the world as a singer, actor, and style icon.

Harry's fans have watched him grow as an artist and a person over the years. Today, he's known for using his voice to do more than just sell out concerts and make albums. He's using it to make a difference in the world by spreading messages of equality, acceptance, and kindness.

In His Words

"As you grow up and **experience** more of the world, you become more comfortable with who you are."

— Interview with Timothée Chalamet for *i-D* magazine from November 2018

Harry has spoken often about the importance of being authentic, or real, in his music and his life. He's **inspired** many of his fans to be their most authentic selves too.

5

MAKING THE BAND

Harry Edward Styles was born in England on February 1, 1994. His parents—Anne Twist and Desmond Styles—divorced, or ended their marriage, when Harry was a kid. After the divorce, Harry lived with his mom and his older sister, Gemma.

Harry loved **performing** from an early age. He was even the lead singer of a band when he was in school. His mother believed in him, and she told him to try out for a TV show called *The X Factor*. During the show, Harry was put in a group with four other boys to form a band called One Direction.

In His Words

"I think the typical thing is to come out of a band like that [One Direction] and almost feel like you have to apologize for being in it … But I loved my time in it."

— Interview with *Vogue* magazine from November 2020

One Direction came together in 2010. The boys in this band didn't have success on *The X Factor* as solo artists, but they became very successful together! Shown here are the members of the band. From left to right, they're Niall Horan, Liam Payne, Zayn Malik, Louis Tomlinson, and Harry Styles.

BOY BAND SUCCESS

One Direction quickly became the most popular boy band in the world. Their first album, *Up All Night,* came out in 2011. It **debuted** at the top of the Billboard 200 chart, which ranks the 200 most popular albums in the United States.

The group's next three albums—*Midnight Memories* (2012), *Take Me Home* (2013), and *Four* (2014)—also debuted at the top of the Billboard 200 chart. This was the first time in history a band did that with its first four albums. Harry and the other members of One Direction had become music superstars!

In His Words

"I think having that [time in One Direction] is kind of priceless. There is very much a respect between all of us ... And that is something that you can't really undo. And you know, it's like a very deep love for each other."

— Interview with Zane Lowe for Apple Music from May 2022

In 2013, the movie *One Direction: This Is Us* came out. This movie shows what life was like for the members of the band at that time while also showing parts of a concert in London, England.

A NEW DIRECTION

One Direction came out with their fifth album, *Made in the A.M.*, in 2015. The next year, the members of the band announced they were taking a break. They wanted to try making music as solo artists.

In 2017, Harry came out with his first solo album, *Harry Styles*. As a solo artist, Harry continued to have success. *Harry Styles* debuted at the top of the Billboard 200 chart, and Harry's first solo tour broke records for how quickly it sold out. His fans were excited to see him live, and he traveled the world on tour from 2017 to 2018.

In His Words

"We have a choice, every single day that we wake up, of what we can put into the world, and I ask you to please choose love every single day."

— Speech given during a concert in May 2017

Many One Direction fans continued to support Harry as a solo artist. He also reached new fans with his new music.

THE HITS KEEP COMING

Harry came out with his next solo album in 2019. *Fine Line* was another huge success that put Harry at the top of the Billboard 200 chart once again. The song "Watermelon Sugar" was on this album. It became Harry's first solo song to top the Billboard Hot 100 chart, which ranks the most popular songs in the United States.

Harry's third solo album, *Harry's House*, came out in 2022. Harry topped both the Billboard 200 and Hot 100 charts again with this album and its hit song "As It Was."

In His Words

"I just want to make stuff that is right, that is fun, in terms of the **process**, that I can be proud of for a long time, that my friends can be proud of, that my family can be proud of, that my kids will be proud of one day."

— Interview with *Better Homes and Gardens* magazine from April 2022

Harry won a Grammy Award—the most famous prize in the music business—for "Watermelon Sugar" in 2021. In 2023, he won two Grammy Awards for *Harry's House*, including Album of the Year.

TPWK

One of the songs Harry helped write for *Fine Line* is called "Treat People With Kindness." Those words are very important to Harry. They've become a kind of slogan for him—a phrase that shows what he stands for. Harry has sold shirts with this slogan on them, and some of the money has gone toward helping certain groups, including the **LGBTQ+ community**.

In 2019, Harry helped create a website that spreads positive messages. People could visit the website to read something kind about themselves. Part of each message was "TPWK," which stands for "Treat People With Kindness."

In His Words

"Small changes end up making a big difference … It's about being a lot nicer to each other rather than, 'Don't do this, or don't do that, not this yes that.' It's just saying, 'Treat people with kindness,' you know."

— Interview with *Music Week* magazine from December 2019

Harry believes in treating people with kindness, and he also believes we should treat ourselves with kindness. **Mental** health is very important to him. He's been open about how helpful it can be to talk to someone when you're going through a hard time. By being open about his mental health, he's helped others be more open about theirs.

A SAFE SPACE

Harry knows that his voice is powerful. One of the ways he uses it is to call attention to the importance of seeing and loving other people for who they really are. This is especially important for members of the LGBTQ+ community. At his concerts, he's given some members of that community a chance to come out—to publicly take their place as part of the LGBTQ+ community—and be supported.

Harry also makes a difference though his clothing. By wearing dresses and sparkly, bold clothes, he's helping do away with **gender stereotypes** that are harmful for both men and women.

In His Words

"How can you say young girls don't get it? They're our future. Our future doctors, lawyers, mothers, presidents, they kind of keep the world going."

— Interview with *Rolling Stone* magazine from April 2017

dress worn by
Harry on the cover
of *Vogue* magazine

Harry's concerts are often seen by his fans as a safe space
where they can be themselves. Many of his fans are young girls,
women, and members of the LGBTQ+ community.
It's not always easy for them to find safe spaces.

CAUSES HE CARES ABOUT

Over the years, Harry has raised money for many causes that are close to his heart. In 2013, Harry began working with Trekstock. This is an organization, or group, that helps young adults with **cancer**. In 2020, he helped raise money to fight the **COVID-19 pandemic** by selling shirts on his website.

Harry also raises money through his concerts. Some of the money he makes by touring is used to support causes he cares about. These causes include women's health, gun safety, and voting rights. Harry's Love On Tour concerts raised more than $6.5 million from 2021 to 2023.

In His Words

"I think it's a time for opening up and learning and listening … I've been trying to read and educate myself so that in 20 years I'm still doing the right things and taking the right steps … I think it's just a time right now where we could use a little more kindness."

— Interview with *Vogue* magazine from November 2020

The Life of
Harry Styles

1994
Harry Styles is born in England on February 1.

2010
Harry tries out for *The X Factor* and becomes part of One Direction.

2011
One Direction **releases** their first album, *Up All Night*.

2012
One Direction releases the *Midnight Memories* album.

2013
One Direction's album *Take Me Home* comes out, the movie *One Direction: This Is Us* comes out, and Harry begins working with Trekstock.

2014
Harry makes *Four* with the rest of One Direction.

2015
One Direction releases *Made in the A.M.*

2016
Harry and the other members of One Direction take a break from the band.

2017
Harry's first solo album is released, and he acts in the movie *Dunkirk*.

2019
Harry releases *Fine Line*.

2021
Harry wins his first Grammy Award and acts in the movie *Eternals*.

2022
The album *Harry's House* is released, and Harry acts in *Don't Worry Darling* and *My Policeman*.

2023
Harry wins two Grammy Awards, including Album of the Year.

Whether he's part of a band or going solo, Harry knows how to stay busy!

NO LIMITS

Harry is more than just a singer. He's known for his style and is often on the covers of magazines. He can even be seen on the big screen! The first movie Harry acted in, *Dunkirk*, came out in 2017. Since then, he's been in movies such as *Eternals*, which came out in 2021, and *Don't Worry Darling* and *My Policeman*, which both came out in 2022.

Harry Styles has shown his fans that there are no limits to who someone can be. He's also shown them that the most important thing they can be is kind.

In His Words

"It's important to stand up for what we think is right. I would love for my views to come through in the music I make and the things I do. That's a very powerful way that we can use our voices."

— Interview with Timothée Chalamet for *i-D* magazine from November 2018

Be Like Harry Styles!

Treat people with kindness. This can be as simple as holding the door open for someone or asking someone who looks lonely to sit with you and your friends at lunchtime.

Find your own slogan—like Treat People With Kindness—and write it down. Share it with others to spread a positive message.

Make wherever you are a safe space for others by making everyone feel included.

Speak kindly to others—and to yourself.

If someone is having a bad day, write them a note or card telling them something you like about them.

Raise money for causes you care about. Maybe you can have a concert for a cause at your school!

If you hear someone saying that something is only for boys or only for girls, remind them that gender stereotypes hurt everyone.

It might not be easy to start a band or star in a movie, but that's not the only way to be like Harry Styles! All you need to do is be kind.

GLOSSARY

cancer: A sometimes deadly sickness in which cells grow in a way they should not, often forming tumors, or growths, that harm the body.

COVID-19 pandemic: An event that began in China in 2019 in which a disease that causes breathing problems, a fever, and other health issues spread rapidly around the world and made millions of people sick in a short period of time.

debut: To introduce something to the public for the first time.

experience: To do or see something or to have something happen to you.

gender stereotype: An idea that's formed about all people of a certain gender, such as all men or all women, that's often untrue or only partly true.

inspire: To move someone to do something great.

LGBTQ+ community: A group made up of people who see themselves as a gender different from the sex they were assigned at birth or who want to be in romantic relationships that aren't only male-female. LGBTQ stands for lesbian, gay, bisexual, transgender, and queer or questioning.

mental: Relating to the mind.

perform: To entertain people by singing or acting.

process: A series of actions that lead to a certain result.

release: To make something available to the public.

solo: Relating to something done alone.

FOR MORE INFORMATION

WEBSITES

Billboard: Harry Styles

www.billboard.com/artist/harry-styles/

The official *Billboard* magazine website offers a short look at Harry's life and lists of where his albums and songs have ranked on the charts.

Harry Styles

www.hstyles.co.uk/

Harry's official website has links to listen to his music, learn more about his tours, and watch his music videos.

BOOKS

Anderson, Kirsten. *Who Is Harry Styles?* New York, NY: Penguin Workshop, 2023.

Huddleston, Emma. *Harry Styles.* Lake Elmo, MN: Focus Readers, 2021.

Schwartz, Heather E. *Harry Styles: Pop Star with an X Factor.* Minneapolis, MN: Lerner Publications, 2023.

INDEX